Broken Publications

A

Pacific Northwest

Independent Publisher

© 2011 by Jennifer-Crystal Johnson

All rights reserved. No part of this book may be reproduced or transmitted in any form by any means, electronic or mechanical, including photocopying and recording, without the prior written permission of the publishers, except by a reviewer who may quote brief passages in a review to be printed in a newspaper, magazine, or journal.

First printing: October 2011.

ISBN 978-0-9828587-3-8

Printed and bound in the United States.

The Heart Series art and image manipulation by Jennifer-Crystal Johnson, rendered in black and white for this book. To purchase prints or see full-color versions, please visit:

http://www.zazzle.com/brokenpoet/

Original cover art by Malinda Ayers Cooper © 2011

To my family:

I couldn't ask for a better one.

I love you all very much,

and thank you for

putting up with my insanity

and

sharing in my joy.

A big thank you goes out to my good friend, Malinda, who painted the cover of this book.

Strangers with Familiar Faces

By Jennifer-Crystal Johnson

Part 1:

She is Me, I am She

Lunging Thoughts

The quiet girl sitting in a booth
all by herself, sipping a cup of
coffee, lighting another cigarette,
writing down any phrase, any
thought that happens to appear
right before her eyes,
right in front of her face,
lunging at her,
attacking her,
forcing its way into her brain....

So, obligingly she sits and writes
and pauses her thoughts only
when she needs to. Sometimes, she
thinks too much. Sometimes, while
driving in her ugly brown car,
she loses her way in a familiar place
because, although she is focused
on traffic and signs,
she's not really quite there in the car.

She is drifting away
on thoughts, feelings, emotions;
she is slipping, sliding, falling,
regressing further
into herself.

Crumbling

Beat her down;
lean on her until
she finally gives,
collapsing to nothing
but bits and pieces
of a complex puzzle

With no one there
to put her back together,
to build her up again
so they can beat her down
once more…

Dead and then
brought back to life
by everyone
who's ever needed her
for anything at all

Only to find that
her mind is no longer
complete or awake;
the purity gone,
the innocence lost

Her honesty stolen from her
and trampled upon
by so many friends
so many lovers
so many strangers
simply to redeem
their nonexistent

Dignity.

Needing Change

White figure cloaked in black
without purpose or direction
or any means or ambition to
begin where she left off. Since
the physical won't change, she
changes what she can and
makes it better, but
the comfort of old habits
won't let her be renewed
and she is left enraged and
frustrated with herself for being
unable to control....

Let yourself fall
backwards,
away from what you thought you knew
and open yourself
to feel something new.

No Feelings

Sickly little girl
all dressed up in grunge,
looking through those sullen eyes
at what we call the world

She doesn't understand
or even know what she feels,
so how should she explain?

There seems to be
no course of action
logical to take.
What's the next step
when she doesn't feel like doing anything?

Sleep can be good, but
she doesn't get enough of that.
The little that does find her
is filled with empty dreams,
a hollow
uninviting cold
that stretches out the seams
holding her world together.

Sometimes reality
doesn't seem real at all.

Fragile Thoughts

Tall and thin
And cloaked in black
And surrounded
By mist
And steam
And smoke

And fiery lights
Are reflected inside
The blue, piercing,
Smoldering anger
Trapped in her eyes

Her stature
Is graceful
Yet strong
But her mind
Seems fragile
So utterly unsure

And though she looks
Like all fire and hell
Her vulnerable innocence
Can still be traced
Through those fiery eyes
To her soul

Venomous Love

Such a shy,
mild-mannered girl,
but when too many buttons
have been pressed
too many times
in short succession,
she, too, can lose patience
and break just a little.

She wears a calm mask
but inside she screams;
with passionate fire,
she'll let out her rage
in the form of
razor-sharp words

She'll spit them at you
like glittering, venomous love…

And there is nothing you can do
to save your dying soul.

Ambivalent

Well, here we are again.

She is disappointed in one and
hopeful for another,
but doesn't want to feel because
it gets her into trouble.

Torn between trying and not,
between being true and
no longer caring.

Between what she really wants
what she wants to want
and what she
seems to want.

She is ambivalent.

The Plot Thickens

Twisting and
unfolding,
there's a complete
lack of surprise.

As the story continues
the plot will thicken;
many trials
will have to be overcome
by our main character.

Her life has become
this endless cycle of
drama
then boredom
then excitement
and more drama.

She has a knack for
fixing other people…
but the real challenge lies
in fixing herself.

Honest Liar

Did you hear about the girl
that wanted to run away,
that wanted to
see it all,
meet everyone,
be everywhere,
know everything?

She died last week.

She died because
she realized
that life just happens
all the time,
that she has found
her purpose
and that made her
someone else.

So this girl she used to be
went away,
far away,
but every now and then,
she comes back to say hello,
to visit for a while,
and to let me know,
to remind me

That I was once
a whore,
a poet,
a restless loner with
too many friends....

A heartless lover,
a beautiful slut,
an honest liar
and a faithful cheater.

A selfish, giving,
needy, careless,
gorgeous woman-child....

I miss her.

See What Becomes

An empty shell
she walked alone
her personal hell
inflicted by him

She never tried
to make him change
because she feared
that angry cage

Always pissed off
even when he was glad
so nothing she did
could be *not* bad

She tried and she tried
to make things alright
but his anger remained
and her spirit died

Then they were apart
for a little while
she realized everything
and now sits with a smile

Because now she has found
who she's been all along
and she knows he can't steal that;
he can't take her song

Reunited with passion
and happy again,
all the things that he stole
she has somehow regained

And when he returns,
she will gladly wait
to see what becomes
of this love, pain, and hate.

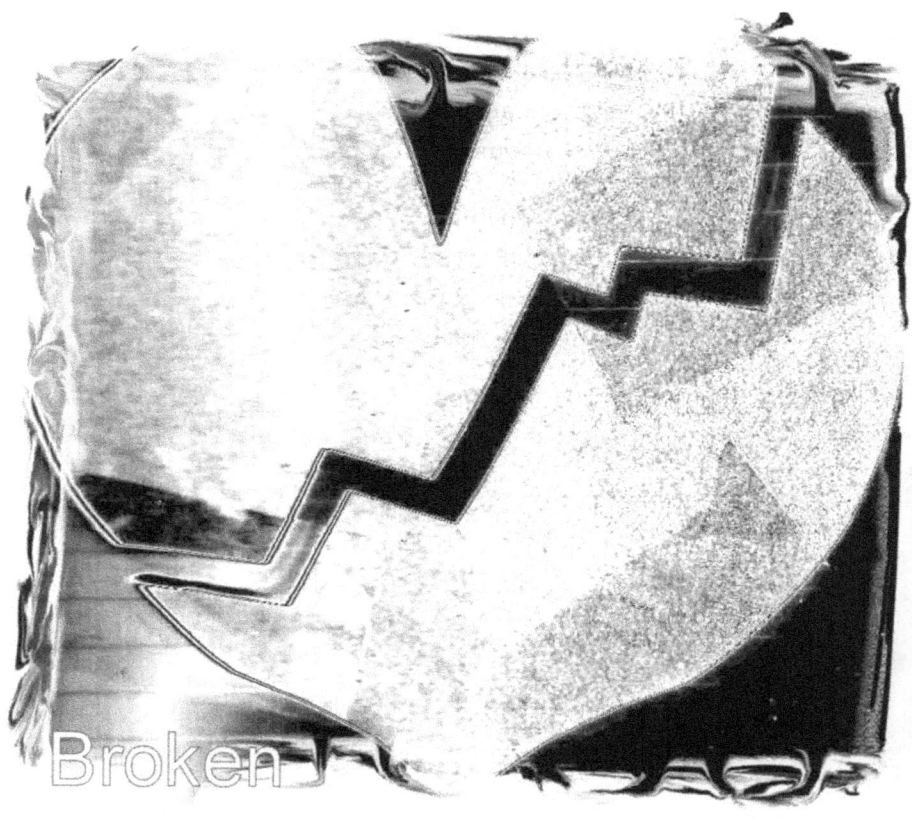

Turn the Page

And they told her before
That he was no good;
she refused to listen.

She never thought he would
treat her so badly.
As she smiles sadly
her battle's begun.

She has to be strong
for herself and her child
can't let this go on,
it's not good; it's not right.

She hopes all the time
and with all of her heart
that she'll find the courage
to tear love apart.

She has to turn the page
and start over again;
she can't live her life
in this fear and pain…

If she stays his wife
it will drive her insane.

Lonely Face

And there she was
The quiet night
Sitting still
Not there, not quite

And there it lay
The broken vase
The water spilled
It met her gaze
And eyes stared
Into other eyes
As flowers framed
Their pretty face

The knees buckle
The fingers shake
And all the while
She's wide awake

Without a sound
It screams at her
And still, somehow
The voice is heard

Yet through the screams
The laughter rings
Mocking dreams
The silence sings

Many nights
Were spent this way
When all the light
Seems to dissipate
But soon the eyes
Evaporate
And all that's left
Is her lonely face

Part 2:

Chaos and Fear

The Butterfly

Once upon a time in a little box lived a tiny caterpillar.
She loved to eat, and one day consumed
an obscene amount of food and then hid herself away
in a lovely cocoon.

She slept for a long time,
dreaming of being beautiful and free.

When she woke up, she felt different.

Breaking open her cocoon,
she emerged to see the sky, the trees,
a beautiful day.

When she looked ahead and tried to fly away,
a beautiful creature stared back at her, leaving her
breathless and in awe.

As she moved, the other moved;
as she turned, the other turned.

How peculiar.

Spreading her wings,
ready to take flight,
the other did the same.

And, as the beautiful butterfly
lifted herself up on the wind,
she collided head-on
with the other.

Awaking in the dark, the beautiful butterfly shivered.
Behind her, the other was still there, echoing her movements.

She turned away from it and took flight,
learning that flying toward herself
is an easy way to die.

The price of vanity.

Reflection

It said to her,
"Look up.
I'm beautiful,
and I'm a reflection
of you."

It smiled down and
it lit the way,
and as she began to cry,
it began to rain.

Tears streamed down and
thunder crashed,
and suddenly she
felt the urge
To fly away forever,
maybe go somewhere
more beautiful than she
and take it in
in gasps of awe
without ever knowing
that it wasn't real.

She can feel her bones here,
the weight of all her sorrow,
jabbing at her body and
beating it into submission.

So when it smiles,
it smiles inside
where no one else can see,
and so does she.

New World

And then one day it came to be
that there was nothing left to say.

Thoughts collapsed and feelings burned,
all the world stood cold and gray.

Then a tiny seed emerged,
and then somehow it grew.

This is the beginning of
the new world that is you.

The Stranger

Expectantly,
she glances around the room.
It's filled with strangers,
but not hers.

He never appears
when she wants him to.

She's tired of this game,
the endless confusion.

Emotions are fragile;
they can disappear
at any given moment,
or shift into something else.

As fleeting as they are,
she wishes she could have
just a little more time
with her ghost,
her stranger.

He calls her his poet.

The Poet

So she wonders, once again:
Is there anyone like me?
She thought there might've been
for a little while....

The poet meets a stranger
and they spend their time together,
hours of conversation,
raw communication,
for days and then months

And she finds herself falling,
but has nowhere to land.

He tears her heart in two;
she, no longer his poet,
and he, no longer her stranger.

She sheds her tears
then slowly becomes numb.

She locks her heart away again,
safely inside the cave
that houses her innermost dreams.

Her stranger was never really hers,
and for a little while
she lied to herself,
for she was never
his poet.

Misunderstandings

Sometimes so confused
so sensitive, abused
without the feeling of
ever being used

She cracks a joke and he
tends to take it as
more than just a joke
so angry then, and why

Maybe she just takes it
a little bit too far
and maybe she can't fake it
as well as she once thought

With everything he sees
she's surprised her humor
still remained unknown,
maybe even disappointed

She doesn't want to piss him off
even more than he always is
so she keeps her mouth shut
for the time being, at least

Eventually he'll see everything,
at least she hopes so.

Dangerous Question

Just barely beginning
to open up,
making her nervous,
the thought of more.

But she knows not why
nor does she try
to contemplate the answer
to such a dangerous
and confusing question
in her mind.

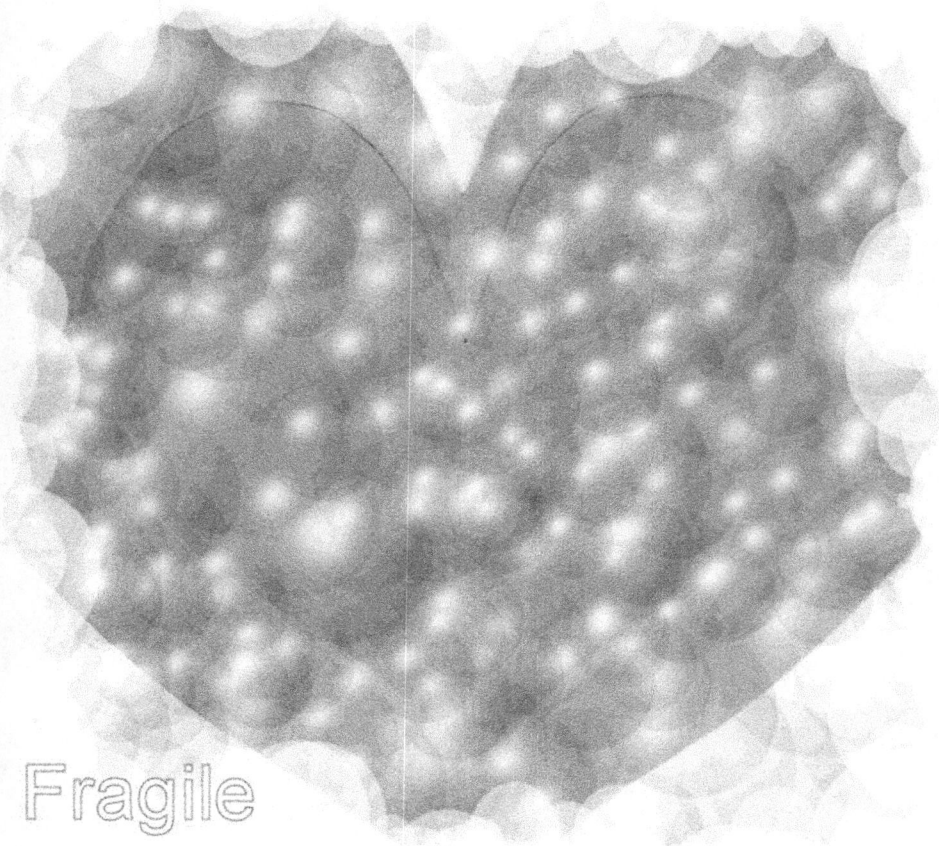

Misperception

And so, it came about
that the whole world was against him.
He felt he was
the unwanted child
that he had feared being.

However, this was not
in actuality
the case, for
everyone loved and missed him.

Just the one that
mattered most
didn't seem to.

She tried not to;
when he came into her thoughts,
she pushed him out.

However,
she never told him this,
so he went on believing
that she hated him.

She couldn't make herself forget
or lie to herself forever.
Her guilt was overwhelming,
and she planned to
pay her debt
for trying to
leave him behind.

Who is she?

She is so many things;
she's a writer, a musician,
a poet, and sometimes
an actress, a performer....

She's frustrated
but relieved;
happy but sad;
stressed out and calm,
crazy and sane....

Stable but restless,
rational and reckless,
she's trapped in her freedom.

Insanely normal
with mediocre
eccentricities....

She is so many things.

Wanting More

She will remain
trapped in this cycle
of confusion
as long as she still
searches for
that unknown.

The highway beckons,
calls to her like
the soft whisper of
her lover
when he is left

wanting

more.

And the weakness,
the lack of will,
the inability to resist....

Giving in
again.

Buried Treasure

And there she sits,
a strange concoction
of calm, quiet contentment
mingling with
the ever-present
mood swings of
a woman.

The children
seem to bring out the worst
when their ears
have been cut off
and buried somewhere,
like a treasure.

If she can find
that X on
a nonexistent map,
if only she could
sew their ears back on,
there would be peace,
she would have quiet
with a sprinkling of
no more worries,
no more anxiety.

Their bickering is like
a bullet,
fired at her thoughts,
shattering them
irreparably.

Undertow of Sadness

She sits with an undertow of sadness in her soul,
every now and then a trickle of it shows,
waiting for redemption,
waiting for salvation,
waiting for the blackness to subside....

Her colors fade so fast
when she allows herself to feel
and emotions are an angel and a demon at their best
without logic, without reason
trying to understand what's going on inside
is a trip through hell and back, in and of itself.

So she waits for the tears to stop,
slowly but surely feeling her heart
crumble into pieces again,
fall apart and unravel,
the decay of her soul and her sanity
falling in around her
and taking over everything....

How did this happen?

With one wrong path chosen,
one mistake made,
the spiral begins and gains momentum
hours pass, as she contemplates her life:
the choices she's made, the mistakes,
the ceaseless and persistent sense
that she will remain broken
no matter how much duct tape
holds her together….

She's tired, fighting the sadness…
exhausted beyond recognizing herself,
falling backwards into the arms
of darkness and depression,
the same black world she knew before
seems somehow inviting in its painful presentation,
drawing her in
making her want to bleed nothingness,
feel nothing…
be nothing.

The positive bubble around her is gone,
No longer protecting her from
The agony she knew before…
It all comes crashing down around her,
The safe little world she tried to build.

When there's nothing but pain in sight,
How can she find the motivation,
The drive, or the ambition
To keep going even though the road ran out?
Persevere, persevere,
But how?
Does this, too, have a reason?
Is this undertow of sadness
Pulling her down to where she belongs?

Are the windows to her soul
Meant to portray
A beautiful world, built through sheer will,
With and underlying darkness as its foundation?

Soon, emptiness and numb
Will wrap their loving arms around
This somewhat damaged heart...
The tears that escape are her emotion,
Her ability to feel....
With every heartache, it gets worse,
Takes longer to recover,
Her resilience fleeing with those tears.

Does it really mean she isn't real
If she can no longer feel?

Conflicted

Helpless hands
Twisting, turning
Disconnected
Eyes averted

Lonely lips
Parting, sealing
Puzzled drivel
Endless drizzle

Hopelessly gullible
Helplessly fallible
Caressing her pain
Seems so close to insane

But not close enough to tame

Thirsty souls
Reeling, restless
So retracted
So distracted

Hungry solitude
Clawing, writing
Souls rejected
Hearts conflicted

Empty solitude
Squirming, churning
Souls reflected
Hearts rejected

All within one body

Untitled

Nearing the edge
Of sanity

And every dream
Flashes before her
With a pure
Intensity

The beauty of

Reality

Inside out

Part 3:

The Self and its Perceptions

Lessons in Humanity

Sitting here poring over the past writings of an immature girl… she was such a basket case, drama queen, unbalanced and beautiful. I can't help but to think that maybe, just maybe, I should be starting fresh, beginning again with the words that form now as opposed to the ones that were written so long ago.

She pesters me. As if it's important to be in a book.

The learning experiences are ones that everyone has, however, and this is why she wants to be read.

We're never the same person twice.

Every experience, every lesson… every little disappointment and major heartbreak, every friend, every enemy, every time you have an epiphany… it's all important.

Well. If you learn from it, anyway. If you choose to ignore it or just do the same stupid shit over and over then obviously it's not done its job yet.

Humanity 101: Lessons from falling on your face.

It's unfortunate that some of us have such a difficult time learning from the mistakes of our predecessors.

Or is the problem that our predecessors just don't acknowledge our ability to learn…?

Numb

The Death Card

After a while, she was always drawing the Death card.

Granted, she wasn't a skilled tarot reader, but she knew that there was more to it than coincidence. That was why they always matched her life so well.

Once she got over the fact that it flat out said death and evaluated the meaning of the card itself, she knew that she needed a life changing alteration to happen.

She also knew she had tried. He'd played on her guilt for over a year and she couldn't take it anymore. Wasn't it about time to move on? All she had ever really wanted was to be happy and loved.

In the end, isn't that what everyone wants?

Perceived Inadequacy

She took her leather jacket off, as if she needed to be lighter to write. (She kept overhearing conversations about college and learning to be a doctor. How inadequate she felt.)

But, even with this discouragement, she knew that she would do something great. She would write, and be a mother. Maybe she would find a way to go back to school to study creative writing and psychology. Maybe she would start talking to high school students about not getting married too young, or even about how to be published authors.

She wasn't sure how to convey to people that she wasn't stupid just because she only had a GED.

Loneliness

And when all was said and done,
the only one remaining
was the lonely girl,
sitting in the corner
by herself.

And, as was once said,
loneliness is
the human condition.

Lost Luster

Where once there was
a mystery of sorts,
a calm wonder
at the silence,
a silly fascination
with the quirky traits
that inhabited
the magical people....

Now there is
just simply silence
or the mediocre chatter
of the diner.

The silence itself,
once so awe-inspiring
and so mysterious,
is now an empty one.

The War Inside

Raging battles
of mixed emotions
occupy the mind,
and the thought
of simple peace
and contentment
seems too far away
to ever be a reality.

The war inside
is hidden well,
and rarely ever
does it surface;
never is
the extent of the damage
seen by anyone.
Signs are posted,
bits and pieces
shimmer through,
but never really surface.

Torn in too many
different directions,
the battle continues,
never ending,
and never seen.

The Scratch of Pen and Paper

The daughter can hear her mother weeping late at night, the scratch of pen and paper as a background to the pain. So much for one person, and without anyone to turn to for a shoulder to cry on.

You want to know about your father? This is what he did to you.

The finger-shaped brown bruises still linger in the mother's mind, and she feels a million different things she can't explain.

Always feels as though she has to be strong. She never loses her composure in the midst of other people, but 2:00 am seems to be her breaking point. Alone, soul bleeding, the crudely fastened bandages of temporary relief fall away, leaving sores open and gaping.

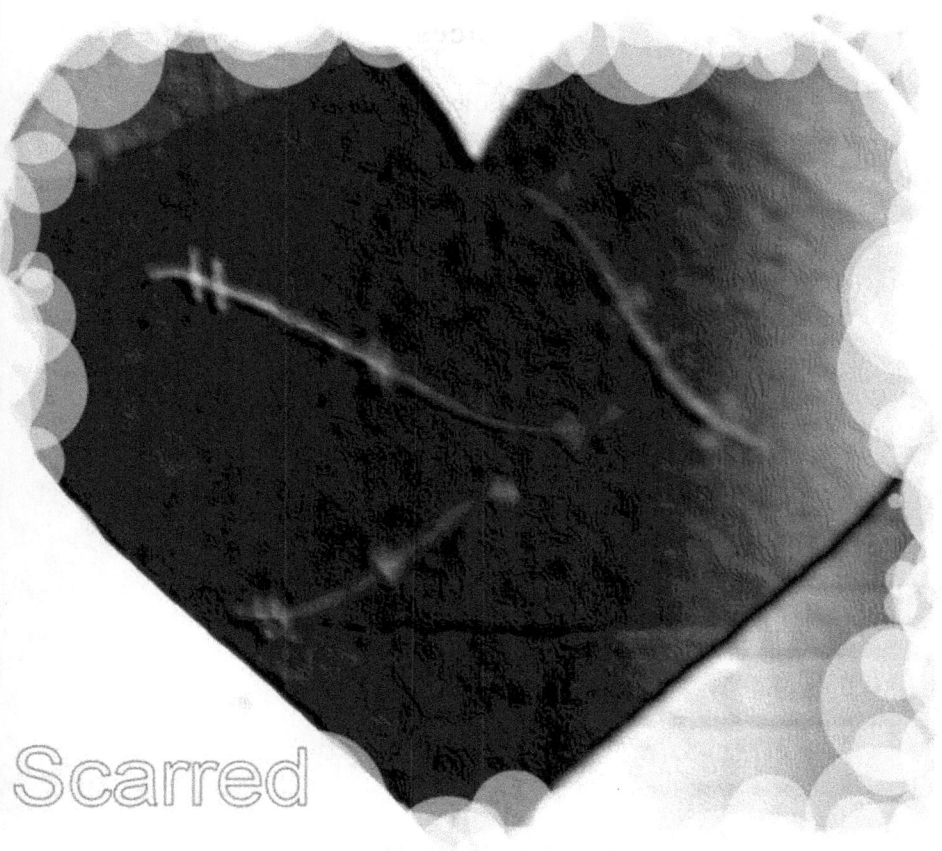

Voices

Voices
conjure images
that do not
match the face.

How can
something beautiful
become
such a disgrace?

The wondering,
the awe,
the confusing
way it goes....

And where
will all these
situations
take us?

No one knows.

Consciousness

To feel the body
dissolve
and turn into
ashes....

To be blown away
by a strong wind,
never bound
by the physical,
only flying
above the whole world....

A sense of freedom
must be achieved
one way or another,
to even out
the sense of
being trapped
in an

Unwanted
situation.

Instructions

Here is your life.

Here is what you need
to survive.

Now, if you break it,
you have to fix it…

So here is some glue.

What you do
is entirely up to you,
so be careful
what you choose.

Heartbeat

The brake lights
are the
heartbeat
of the interstate
during
rush hour

Blinking steadily
on and off
as traffic
slowly pulsates

South
on I-5

The Color of a Failing Soul

Swirling colors
the rainbow personified
a soul, free spirit
has let too many
painful experiences
alter the colors of
its light

Mixed up and stirred
shaken, bruised, churning
broken, repaired
ripped up again

Now the rainbow
is a murky gray
with random slices of color
brightness in the abyss
the colors cutting
through the gray
like the sun does
through thick storm clouds

Can't undo the mash-up
can't reverse the gray

But maybe
just maybe
the color hasn't gone away
and the slices can expand
grow more powerful
than the
decadence
of a
colorless soul

Is there a return from this
gray fog,
the decaying color
that has become of
what was once
so bright and beautiful

Innocence has not
been maintained

Gray is
the color
of a
failing soul

Cycle

Helpless hands
twisting, turning
disconnected
eyes averted

Lonely lips
parting, sealing
puzzled drivel
endless drizzle

Hopelessly gullible
helplessly fallible
caressing your pain
seems so close to insane
but not close enough to tame

Thirsty souls
reeling, restless
so retracted
so distracted

Hungry solitude
clawing, writhing
love rejected
hearts conflicted

Empty solitude
squirming, churning
souls reflected
hearts rejected

All within
one body

Part 4:

The Sun, the Rain, and the Rainbow

Chapter One

Somehow, the rain
met up with the sun
and they had a child and
named it Rainbow

The child was born
between light and dark
and torn between the same
ambivalent,
two opposites;
not knowing where to turn.

Stormy and moody,
Mother Rain sings
on pavement and
the tops of umbrellas…

While Father Sun
reflects upon
that same pavement,
erasing Mother's song.

Chapter Two

So the Sun asked the Rain
"Why do we get along so rarely?"
The Rain blots out the Sun,
the Sun dries up the Rain,
the two fight constantly;
they just don't mesh well.

The poor child Rainbow
is hardly ever seen,
hardly ever heard.

Rainbow feels ignored and
useless, unimportant.
No matter how beautiful,
Rainbow is tormented
by her indecisive nature
and the constant battle
Raging inside.

Rainbow tries so hard
to belong, to fit in,
to be accepted and loved,
and still, she feels ignored.

So the Rain says to the Sun,
"We should try to get along,
but I don't know
if that's possible."

Mother Rain plays a part
as well as Father Sun,
but Rainbow can't seem
to find much of their love
anywhere in sight.

Can't seem to find herself, either.

So Rainbow is
constantly confused.

Chapter Three

And there was a
Tremendous silence,
right after the storm,
when the Sun would
ask the Rain
why she didn't love him.

And the Rain replied
without hesitation,
"We could never
live in peace."

That's just the way it is.

Chapter Four

So the Rain asked the Sun,
"Why do you want
to take my Rainbow away?"

The Sun replied,
"I don't know. I just need
reassurance,
for I am insecure."

The Rain pondered this
for just a moment,
then she said to the Sun,
"I am insecure as well,
and this will make me more so.
Why would you cause
such pain for me,
for you, for *her*?"

The Sun replied quickly,
"Because *you* caused *me* pain."

The Rain began to cry
her icy, painful tears,
covering the world
with her sorrow.

Not even Father Sun
could evaporate these clouds.

Rainbow was hiding.

Mother Rain knew
that she had no choice;
if she wanted to be with Rainbow
she would have to stay,
and make him stay,
no matter how much pain they felt.

Chapter Five

The baby will be
the child called Growth,
where Sun and Rain
must work together.

This will bring them closer,
until they become steam,
and try to stay that way.

Nothing can change that
except for themselves,
so hope exists
That everything will be fine.

Chapter Six

The Sun and the Rain
have come together.
They have made steam,
and the child called Rainbow
is happy again.

She misses the Sun
when he does not shine,
and she misses the Rain
when she leaves her sight.

But now they're together,
just as they should be;
even when they can't see.

They now seem unable
to live without each other,
and, therefore, will stay
just as they are now.

Forever is always,
through good and bad days,
and when they feel
on the verge of breaking,
The child Rainbow
will remind them:

She cannot live
when they are apart.

Chapter Seven

Mother Rain
has learned
the hardest thing
she's ever had to learn.

Rainbow can live
when the Sun isn't there,
for light can be found
everywhere.

When the Sun
burned through the child Rainbow,
Mother Rain knew
that they needed to run.

Rainbow is broken,
unable to mend,
her scars are untreatable
and her mind is bent.

But Mother Rain loves her
more than Rainbow knows,
and would die if it meant
that she would be safe.

The child called Growth
wasn't meant for the Sun;
she was meant for the Rain
and the joy to come.

The Sun has been hiding
away from sight,
not quite all gone,
but not quite as bright.

The Sun has grown cold, though,
unwilling to help
Unwilling to be
a part of their lives,
not even the ways that he could.

So Mother Rain comforts
and reassures
and soaks up tears with
her shirtsleeves.

Rainbow and Growth
have helped mend each other,
and Mother Rain, too;
their love sees them through.

Wounded

Part 5:

The Final Word

Simply Me

Once upon a time,
She was me and I was she,
But did that mean I wasn't me?
I had so many uncertainties.

Anxiety had let me be,
But sadness never felt a need…
To leave.

Some time went by for she and I,
And I and she,
And now, my friends, I guarantee
That she's not me
And I'm not she….

Now, I'm simply me.

Conversations with Myself
establishing the mission

When everything is said and done, what does it all really mean? Does it matter what you went through? Has anyone witnessed it and been altered, improved? What about everything else that you've written? Those things surely don't help people, so why the poetry?

> *The poetry is the soul. The poetry comes from a place of great despair and joy, of emotional manic depressive tendencies. The poetry is like music.*

But why not just write a story to illustrate your meaning? It doesn't make any sense to me. Stories are much more addictive to read.

> *I'm getting there... you can only control certain aspects for so long before it finally snaps back and you open the floodgates. That's what I'm afraid of... though I know I'm a little strange, maybe even a little crazy, I also know my boundaries and what I can and cannot handle. The stories will come in time, at least in story form.*

So really, this is the beginning... these poems, these collections, will be followed up by more in-depth things, things that may or may not be appropriate for most, things that no one wants to admit to knowing or having seen....

> *... Things that people are uncomfortable discussing because it's in their faces every single day but they have no idea what to do about it, or are afraid to say anything. These are things that people who don't know first-hand are too ignorant or too aloof or afraid to fully comprehend ... or want to comprehend. These things need to be busted wide open and the world needs to know that it happens all the time.*

So that's the mission, then. What if it completely fails? I mean, don't you need some sort of plan?

> *The HOW doesn't matter. Only the WHY. The HOW will present itself as it is needed, because that's how it's been for the past several years. I simply communicate, and the rest takes care of itself... the trick is to seize opportunities as they present themselves and, if it's something you truly, truly want, you stick with it... you work your hardest, and you go for it, and it will pay off. There's a lot to be said for perseverance.*

So you're telling me that you have these grandiose ideas, these things you want to communicate with the world, but you don't even know how to go about it?!

> *... Says the inner skeptic....*

No, seriously?! You have no idea what you're doing, and you plan to do it anyway.

> *I wouldn't say I have no idea. I'm still learning... but so is everyone else. I just hope that the lessons don't fall on deaf ears and blind eyes and the whole thing is useless... but it won't be. It'll reach at least a handful of people and send the message I need it to send. Quit being such a pessimist!*

Quit being such an optimist! It's naïve.

> *Fine. So I'm naïve.*

The How, the Why, and I

I originally wrote a poem about this when I was 16. The How always seemed to get in the way of everything I wanted to do… How could I go anywhere if I never figured out how?

Then there were opportunities. Many of them led to very dark places in my past, those little caves that you cover with boulders to keep away from even your closest friends. Cover it up so no one can see.

Then there was an immense period of pain and fear, which I let consume my spirit and had to claw my way back out of. Three years of being trapped, mentally abused, sexually terrorized and manipulated, and otherwise made to feel like a *lesser* human being.

But I was always so fun! I used to be so creative! I used to be so social! I used to be close to my friends and family… what happened?!

… I won't go into detail here, but if you haven't been able to understand through the Rainbow/Sun story poems, then read them again. It's pretty obvious.

Strangers

No idea what to put there, she thinks. She really doesn't want to limit her own personality or potential with a label.

She feels like a stranger in her own skin sometimes. Not belonging, changing so much that she no longer recognizes herself. *What does that mean?*

The only thing she can do is write in her journal about it. It's such an introspective question that talking to anyone seems useless, especially when you know not too many people feel comfortable confronting these huge questions about life and perception and reality and dimension.

The truth is, in any given moment, anyone can be – and probably is – a stranger to themselves. How many people really know who they truly are, what they truly believe? How many people change from moment to moment and have to learn themselves on a constant basis?

You're never the same person twice….

The moments are what count.

Those little moments of epiphany, of love, of passion. The moments that are unmistakably real in a sea of monotonous routine. It seems amplified, but it isn't… it's just not washed over with the numb paint everyone uses to bear their mediocrity and responsibilities.

She looks at her reflection in the mirror, not sure whether to laugh or cry. *Do I know you?* she thinks wryly.

Do I know you?

www.ingramcontent.com/pod-product-compliance
Lightning Source LLC
Chambersburg PA
CBHW071738040426
42446CB00012B/2392